Quick and Fun Learning Activities for Two-Year-Olds

Ina Massler Levin, M.A. & Michael H. Levin, M.A.

Teacher Created Materials, Inc.

Cover Design by Larry Bauer

Made in U.S.A.

Reprinted, 2004

ISBN 1-55734-555-6

Order Number TCM 555

Table of Contents

Introduction

Bubbly, busy, cute, and cranky. Two-year-olds fill our lives with their endearing charm, effervescent energy, and boundless enthusiasm for life. Two-year-olds have mastered the art of saying no, trying our patience, and testing our endurance as parents. But they have also captured our hearts with their ever-growing command of language, their intense desire to please, and their delight in things new to them. Two-year-olds are adorable, challenging, and exhausting. They are also lots of fun to be with.

With great pleasure, we remember our girls when they were two. We took them to the park and the beach, made lots of messes with bubbles and sand, sang the same songs over and over again, and watched with sheer amazement as they grew and flourished. We also remember the times we were exhausted and they screamed for "more" or "again." How well we remembered all of this as we were writing this book!

In realizing that so much has to be done, the activities you will find in this book are geared to families that lead busy lives. The games and projects we suggest will take little preparation and cleanup. Both you and your child will benefit, not only from the interaction these activities are designed to achieve but also from the closeness you will derive.

Our age designation is divided between "younger two" and "older two." A younger two is anywhere from twenty-four to thirty months, and an older two is from thirty to thirty-six months. However, as a parent, you know best which stage of development your two-year-old is in at the time. For instance, if an activity says to have your child repeat a sentence back and she does not, do not despair. She may not be ready for these words yet. Try again in a week or a month. As hard as it is for parents not to push, forcing activities will not get you anywhere with your toddler. When your child is ready to run, jump, or sing, she will. However, their time table will make us appreciate them all the more. When expectations are temporarily forgotten, we can see the world through their eyes. You may find that as you play with your two-year-old, your ability to play will be reawakened. Have fun, both of you!

From Two to Three

The period between twenty-four and thirty-six months is a time of wonderful changes for a child. Below are some of the milestones of that year and an approximate time that these may take place. It is extremely important to remember that each child develops at his or her individual pace.

Physical Development
24 to 30 months—The child will:
improve motor skills
climb everywhere, including places not allowed
play on large playground equipment
kick a ball forward
throw overhand, but not aim
carefully turn one page at a time of a book
take lids off jars and screw them back on
turn doorknobs awkwardly
30 to 36 months—The child will:
like to move continually
like running games
go upstairs alternating feet; go downstairs one foot at a time
jump from any height, not judging the distances correctly
put arms and hands straight out to catch a large ball
scribble and draw
build towers of six or more blocks
take apart and put together objects
turn doorknobs more easily

Intellectual Development
24 to 30 months—The child will:
understand cause and effect in terms of personal behavior

use nearby objects in make-believe games
play house while imitating family situations
listen to recordings of stories and songs
remember sequence and may be able to retell stories
recognize familiar signs in environment
become more interested in children's television shows
follow two-step commands
use two-word sentences
refer to self by name
enjoy learning names for new objects
use words to make requests
have a vocabulary of more than 200 words
30 to 36 Months—The child will:
begin to classify objects into general categories
become more skilled with puzzles
be more curious while listening to books and watching television
remember and follow three-step commands
create two-to-three word sentences, including verbs
begin using past tense and plurals
question names of objects and repeat them
connect names and uses of objects
understand relative size (big and small)
have a vocabulary of more than 500 words

Safety Concerns

Where your child is concerned, safety is of the utmost importance. The activities in this book have been designed with that in mind. Consider these saftey issues with your two-year-old.

Your little one can climb. He can drag a chair over to get something he wants and climb up. Keep poison, matches, and anything sharp locked up and out of reach. Do not leave his toys on counters where he will have to climb to reach. He can and will. Also be aware that a two-year-old can climb through windows and open doors. Keep them shut and locked.

A two-year-old is curious about everything. He will touch, taste, and smell anything, so take care in what you leave around. When you cook, keep pot handles turned into the stove so he cannot knock them off. If you leave loose change around, he may find it and put it into his mouth. If you are at the park or in the yard, check to see what he has in his hand. A creepy crawlie may easily wind up in his mouth.

Keep outlets covered so he cannot put fingers or objects into the sockets.

Check his toys. Are there any loose pieces? If the box says for ages three and up, it may have to do with the size of the toy parts rather than the fact that the child will find it fun. Explain to him that he cannot put anything into his mouth. Take it away if he does.

Water play can present a whole new set of safety concerns. Never leave your child unattended while playing in or with water.

Every so often take a tour of your two-year-old's environment from his vantage point. Are there sharp corners on a table that might need padding? Do you see cords that when pulled could easily topple a lamp? If you encounter such a situation, correct it now to avoid a possible accident later.

Be very aware of where you are playing. Take care when playing outside because your two-year-old will run into traffic to get a ball. In the house, he may toss a ball hard enough to break a glass.

Anytime you take your two-year-old in the car, even for just a quick trip, strap him into his car seat!

Stuff Around the House

Playing with a two-year-old often involves nothing more than you and your child. However, some of the activities in this book require a few simple materials. It is a good idea to collect the things you may need before you begin an activity. You do not want to frustrate your child and yourself when you begin something and find out you do not have what you need to finish the activity.

Collect the materials as you can. Find a central location to keep them in. We found a laundry basket was the best for storing the hodgepodge that this type of collection creates. It was lightweight, could hold a lot, and had handles for easy transport.

Do not feel that you have to have every item on the list before you begin enjoying playing with your two-year-old. Add to and subtract as necessary. We have not included supplies such as scissors and tape because you probably already have those, but if your office supplies are limited, be sure to keep them replenished.

Although there are activities throughout this book that employ these materials, do not feel that you must use them only in the way they are described. Time, mood, and energy may give you a better idea as to how to use them. Throw this book on the top of the basket. Then, when the mood strikes you, play, improvise, and above all, have fun with your child.

Stuff to Have Around the House

- Pots and pans
- Wooden and metal spoons
- Balls (beach ball, tennis ball, large and small balls)
- Boxes (various sizes, at least one large enough to climb into)
- Laundry basket
- Books
- Tape recorder

- Radio
- CD player
- Tapes and CDs
- Wrapping paper tubes
- Musical instruments (bells, sand blocks, rhythm sticks)
- Hats (all types)
- Dress-up clothes with easy openings

- Old purses, combs, belts
- Bubbles and wand (tightly capped)
- Play dough
- Plastic placemats
- Handkerchief
- Various fabric squares
- Stuffed animals and dolls
- Trucks and cars

- Push toys (wheelbarrow, shopping cart)
- Food coloring
- Pudding mix
- Chunky crayons
- Paper
- Index cards
- Catalogs
- Sidewalk chalk

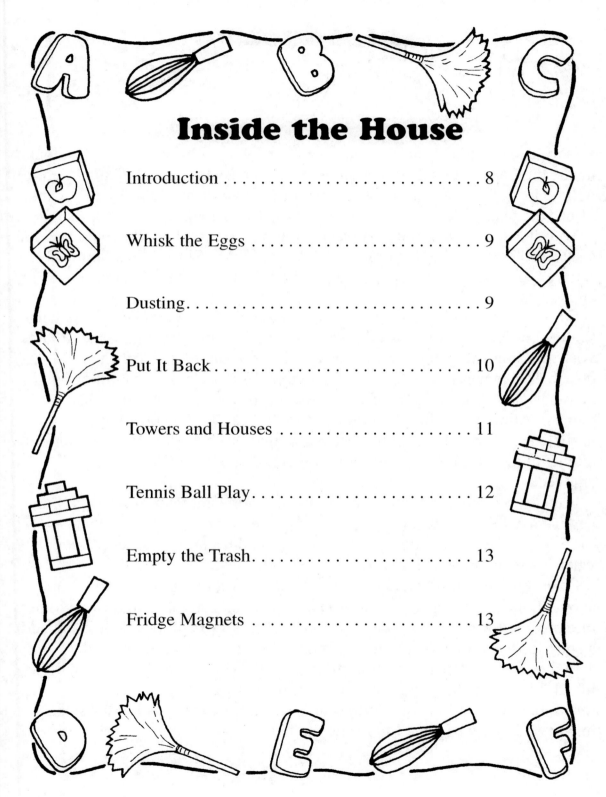

Inside the House

Introduction

During your child's second year the two of you will spend countless hours inside the house. Beside the obvious time spent sleeping and eating, there will be lots of time for playing. Sometimes you will need to stay in because of bad weather. Make the most of this time by playing with your little one.

Your house is one of the best places in the world to play. It should provide a safe and comfortable environment for your child. Since it is a familiar setting, your child will face new experiences with the least amount of apprehension.

By the time your child turns two, your house, of course, should have been safety-proofed. However, since she can move furniture to climb, make sure you store items that you do not want her to have out of sight. If it is possible, give her a large area to run and jump in. A mat on the floor will help out. If you have stairs, she will still need watching or help as she climbs. Allow your child all the freedom you can in the house. We designated a low cabinet in the kitchen as their space. Here we kept not only kitchen things we felt would be fun to play with but added whatever they enjoyed.

If there is an area of the house that you do not want your child to go into, begin early to close the door and tell her, "We do not go in the laundry room." (The room should still be child-proofed because you never know when someone might leave the door open.)

Playing in the house affords an excellent opportunity to teach your child about chores. Making these fun is easy since you can make almost anything into a game for a two-year-old if you do the task right alongside her and add a song to it. As you look at this section, you will see that many of the activities are ones that see a task through to the end. This type of finish-the-job attitude helps build the idea of being responsible. Nevertheless, remember your child is only two years old, and while she is learning, the major goal is to just have fun inside the house.

Whisk the Eggs

Materials

- Bowl
- Eggs
- Wire whisk

Activity

Crack a few eggs into a deep bowl. If you are intent on using the eggs later, crack them yourself. Otherwise, let your two-year-old have a chance at cracking them. There is a fifty-fifty chance that the eggs will wind up in the bowl. There is a greater likelihood that there will be eggshell in the bowl.

Show your child the whisk and how it can mix things. Show her how to mix the eggs, pointing out how the eggs change from two distinct sections of clear liquid and the yolk into a creamy yellow mixture. Once the eggs are mixed, it is up to you to decide how (or if) you are going to use them.

Dusting

Materials

- Dust cloth or feather duster

Activity

Your two-year-old will enjoy helping you dust if you are not too particular about getting every dust streak off the table. Give your child a soft cloth or a feather duster and let him dust away. He really can be helpful when it comes to dusting the rungs of chairs or the legs on tables because he will reach them much more easily than you. Our younger daughter wanted her own feather duster. We bought her a small one with orange feathers. Our house was never so dust free!

Put It Back

Materials

- Out-of-place items
- Words to the song (See below.)

Activity

This is an excellent opportunity to turn putting things away into a real game. If there are toys scattered everywhere, this game becomes too overwhelming. Play it as you go along. Introduce it when it looks like your two-year-old is finished with one toy and about to go to another.

When a few items have accumulated or you have a toy with many pieces, such as blocks scattered, it is time to play "Put It Back." Pick up one of the toys that your two has been playing with and say, "We are going to play a special game called 'Put It Back.' It even has its own song. Each time we are done with a toy, we find out where it goes, and we place it back in the toy box where it belongs. We get to sing as we do this. The fun part is that when we are through we get to play with more toys."

This Is the Way We Put Things Back

(Sing to the tune of "Here We Go 'Round the Mulberry Bush")

This is the way we put things back, put things back, put things back.

This is the way we put things back, and clean up all our toys.

This is the way we put things back, put things back, put things back.

This is the way we put things back, and get another toy.

Towers and Houses

Activity

Materials

• Building blocks

Your two-year-old will enjoy making towers and houses with building blocks just as much as she will like knocking them down. Show your child how to stack the blocks on top of each other so they are balanced and do not fall immediately. Some will fall, and as they do, tell her she will need to pick them up again. Then you can build another house or whatever is today's construction project.

Sitting and building a block town is a good topic to talk about. Ask your child what it is you are building and where it is. Encourage her to bring her dolls, cars, and other toys to the block town. A young two-year-old may build a tower only a few blocks high, but older two's can be more elaborate.

Wooden blocks can be an expensive toy, but they are generally a worthwhile investment. If you do not wish to buy blocks, directions to make simple, inexpensive, light-weight blocks follow.

Directions for Making Blocks

Collect all sorts of cardboard boxes. Shoe boxes with lids, tiny jewelry gift boxes, milk cartons, and food boxes all work well.

Choose some Contact paper with a pattern that you like and cover the boxes with it. You might choose more than one type of paper to cover the boxes.

Make sure that the paper sticks to the outside of the boxes.

Tennis Ball Play

Materials

- Tennis balls
- Container that balls came in
- Large coffee can

Activity

Tennis balls inside the house can be played with in many ways. In fact, a container of tennis balls inside the house can be as much fun as outside. Invest in a can of balls to keep inside so they do not become muddy on the first rainy day.

Quiet Time

This activity works best when your two-year-old is sitting on your lap. Take the container and remove the balls one at a time, counting them as you do. Say, "This is one ball. These are two balls. Now I have three balls. Can you put them back?" Help your child put them back into the container. Count them, "one, two, three," as they are returned.

Rolling

Another way to play with tennis balls is to place the coffee can with the bottom against the wall. Show your two-year-old how to roll the ball on the floor and into the can. As before, count each time you roll the ball. If any of the balls get into the can, count them as you take them out. Remember to make this fun for your child, so do not make the distance the ball has to roll too far away.

Dropping

Set the coffee can upright. Give the tennis balls to your child, one at a time. Show him how to drop the balls into the coffee can and then how to dump them all out to play again. As your two-year-old gets older, you might want to add more balls to drop into the can.

Empty the Trash

Activity

Materials

- Small trash baskets
- Large bag or box

Even emptying the trash from his own room can be fun for a two-year-old. He will not only be accomplishing something but also helping out. Accompany your two on a tour of the house, showing him the trash basket in each room or the ones you designate for him to empty. Take along a large paper sack or a box into which the contents of the trash basket can fit. Show him how to pick up the trash can and not touch anything that is inside of it. Have him dump it into the bag or box. Talk about why we use a trash basket and how important it is to throw dirty items in it. You can then have him accompany you to the outside trash can or bin. Do not forget to watch the trash truck as it picks up the trash from the street.

Fridge Magnets

Activity

Materials

- Refrigerator
- Large magnets

The bottom or the side of your refrigerator can be a great place to play for your toddler. It will keep him busy while you are cooking. Simply give him his own set of magnets to play with. Keep in mind, the magnets he uses should be large enough so he cannot swallow them. They should also be easy to hold and manipulate. It will be fun for him to choose his own magnets to use, especially if you are some place special and would like a souvenir. This way each time he plays with the magnets, you can remind him of the special outing.

There are all types of magnets from which to choose. When your child outgrows them as play toys, use them to display his art work from preschool.

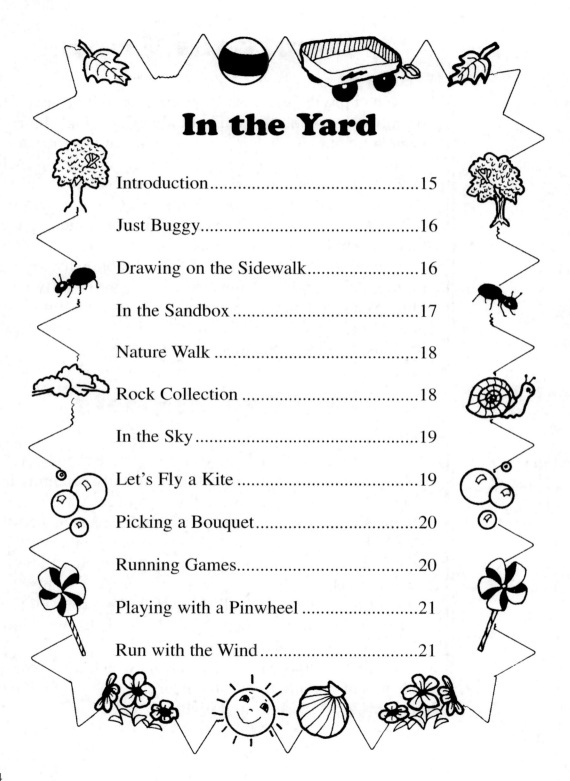

In the Yard

Introduction

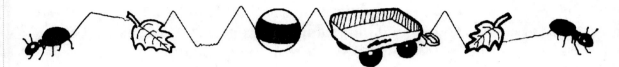

Playing outside is naturally fun for your child. However, after the initial excitement of being outdoors is over, your child might need some encouragement in deciding what to do. The more you help her discover the great outdoors, the more she will want to play and remain outside.

As you do some of the activities in this section, please keep safety in mind. Outdoors should not be frightening to children, but we need to be aware they can be easily hurt. Pointing out places she can get hurt will help her to understand that she needs to be careful. Hold her hand in areas where there is more chance for falling. Do not take her to places where rocks are pointed or not secure. The younger a child is, the more necessary the need for large, broad, flat areas.

Although this section focuses on playing in the yard, most of the activities can easily be done in a park. Take advantage of parks where you live. They often provide large play equipment that encourages physical activity such as climbing and crawling. Remember that your child is still small, and some equipment will prove much too large for her to enjoy. Although she may be willing to climb up the slide, we quickly learned from our own experience that you may have to slide down with her. The social interaction that a park can provide will give both you and your child a chance to play with other two-year-olds and their parents.

You need not always plan every moment of your time outdoors. Your child will soon show you what she enjoys doing. Discover what she likes—with a bit of imagination, both of you will soon be creating your own activities in your yard.

Just Buggy

Materials

- Nonpoisonous bug
- Bug catcher

Activity

With your two-year-old, go on a bug hunt in your yard. What kind of creatures do you see? Can you find a parade of ants, or do you see a grasshopper? Find any harmless bug and use the bug catcher to catch it. (Bug catchers with the magnifying lids work best.) Study the bug. Discuss the color, decide if it has wings, and listen for the sound it makes. Then, set the bug free.

Drawing on the Sidewalk

Materials

- Chalk
- Cement

Activity

On a pretty day, give your two-year-old some chalk and let him have a grand time decorating the sidewalk, patio, or driveway. Encourage him to make large pictures using various colors of chalk. (The type that is made for sidewalks is larger and easier for little hands to use.) Have fun coloring right next to him and be sure to sign your names to your masterpieces.

You can leave the chalk pictures until the next rain or clean them off with a garden hose. Some colored chalks need elbow grease to come off sidewalks, so be sure to decide where it is best to draw.

In the Sandbox

Materials

- Sandbox
- Sand toys (bucket and shovel)
- Plastic pitcher
- Water

Activity

A sandbox is a great investment, but in lieu of a sandbox, the park or a sandy beach will do. Make sure your child has a bucket and shovel ready. There are many types of sand toys, including those that spin when sand is poured into them and those that mold wet sand into wonderful designs. Yet, chances are, your two-year-old will love just sitting and filling the bucket with sand and then dumping it out again. While playing with the sand, the two of you can have an entire conversation as you ask her what she is doing and building.

Another way to play in the sandbox is to bury small objects, like the sand toys, and ask your child to find them.

You will need to keep your eye on the sandbox so your toddler does not eat the sand. You will also want to keep a broom and dustpan handy if the sandbox is on a concrete surface because sand will get out and make the area slippery.

Nature Walk

Materials

• Outdoors

Activity

Take your two-year-old on a nature walk in your own yard or around the block. Hold hands, take a walk, and point out some of the glory of nature. If it is fall, show him the leaves that are turning yellow. If it is summer, point out the flowers in bloom.

A really enjoyable activity with a two-year-old is to find a tree and then walk by it at different times of the year. When you do, point out that the leaves are turning color or dropping. If you see a bird in the tree, point it out to your child and ask him to be very quiet so he can hear it. You might even want to take pictures throughout the year so your child can see the growth of the tree.

Rock Collection

Materials

• Large rocks
• Box or basket

Activity

Little ones like to pick up things. Take advantage of your two-year-old's curiosity. Let him start a rock collection. Even as a young toddler he will pick them up. You can decide if he should keep them or not. As he gets older, take him into the yard and let him look for different types of rocks. Ask him to find smooth or shiny ones. Rocks with special characteristics are among those he should collect. Give him a box or a basket to put the rocks in.

When he has chosen several rocks, help him decide what to do with them. Will they go back into the yard? Will you set up a display right in the yard? Or, will the rocks go in a special spot in his room so he can admire them at his leisure?

In the Sky

Materials

- Blanket

Activity

This activity will work best when your child needs a short rest. Go outside and lie down together on a blanket, side by side. Now look up in the sky, making sure that the sun is not directly overhead or is obstructed from view. Ask your child what she sees up in the sky. Ask her what color the sky is. Does she see any planes or helicopters? Are there any clouds? Encourage her to be aware of looking up and seeing things in the sky.

As an alternative, try this on a warm summer night. How many stars can you see and count? Point out the moon. Let your two-year-old see the difference between the day and night sky.

Let's Fly a Kite

Materials

- A kite
- String
- Windy day

Activity

Assemble a kite according to the directions or buy the type that have wonderfully long tails and dance in the wind. Take your two-year-old into the yard or a park without wires overhead. Tell him you are about to fly a kite in the air with the help of the wind. Show him how you slowly let out the string as the kite takes off.

This is an activity that is best done with more than one grownup since someone has to watch your little one while another runs with the kite. If you have a child who is willing to sit in a stroller while you get the kite up, this will work; otherwise, it is a good idea to include other family members or friends when flying kites.

Picking a Bouquet

Materials

• Flowers for picking

Activity

Take your two-year-old on a walk and pick some flowers. Before you do, be sure to check that the flowers are free of pesticides and thorns. Help your child compose a small bouquet to set into water. Remember, what you view as a weed may bring delight to your child. Wild flowers that grow in the lawn will often make an ideal bouquet for a two-year-old to pick.

Running Games

Materials

• None

Activity

Play running games with your two-year-old. Run next to her, in front of her, behind her, and while holding her hand. Since she will want to run anyway, this is one of those activities that takes advantage of what she already enjoys.

Run to a tree in the yard. Or, teach her how to take turns as she runs first and then waits for you. These games do not have to be competitive. Enjoy running together and encouraging one another.

As an alternative to running, try some other ways to move with your child. Have your child:

• hop on two feet
• walk backwards
• walk on all fours
• turn circles

Playing with a Pinwheel

Activity

Materials

• Pinwheel

Allow your child to select a pinwheel to purchase or make one yourself, following the instructions below. Take your pinwheel out into the yard. Show your child how to make it move by either blowing on it or moving with it. Then, hold the pinwheel and run with it. Give your child a pinwheel and let him make it turn, first by blowing and then by running with it.

We always found the bright, shiny pinwheels were the best. They are captivating to look at, and they are durable. However, sometimes we made our own. Simple directions follow.

Homemade Pinwheel

Directions

1. Make a diagonal cut into each of the four corners of a piece of paper. Make the cuts the same length. Leave a small amount in the center of the paper.
2. Bend one corner into the center of the paper, then the next, until all four corners have formed the pinwheel.
3. Use a pushpin and pin the corners into an eraser that is found on top of a pencil

Run with the Wind

Activity

Materials

• Windy day

Windy days seem to make staying inside almost impossible for two-year-olds. Take advantage of what nature offers; bundle up your toddler and run with the wind.

When you are outside, figure out which way the wind is blowing. Then, take your child's hand and let him lead you as you run with the wind blowing behind you.

Music and Movement

Introduction

Two-year-olds and movement are synonymous. So, why not combine his natural love for movement and music with some directed activities in which you both can participate? And what makes this fun for you is that you get to not only participate, you also get to direct.

As the director, remember a few things. Your child is only two years old. Do not expect perfection. If you want to do ballet when dancing and your child wants to do rock and roll, let him. If he is singing a song and puts in a wrong line or word, do not stop singing to correct him. When he is through, sing the song again with him, using the correct words. There is no need to curb his exuberance because he does not quite have it down right.

Include siblings and other family members when you can. An older brother or sister who can already count might be the perfect one to teach a counting song, while grandparents might be willing participants in a marching parade.

Even at this age music is often soothing. Lullabies you sang to your child as an infant are just as appropriate for your busy two-year-old as his day ends. Making singing a part of your bedtime ritual is highly appreciated.

Music can also be part of the background. Classical music can play softly as your child plays, or favorite tapes of children's music can be played while riding in the car. Again, remember that you will also have to listen to these tapes, so choose carefully. We particularly liked Dan Crow, Sharon, Lois, and Bram, and Raffi. Their music is usually available in children's book and music stores. In the last few years, many recording artists have done albums for children. Our favorite—we give it as a two-year-old baby gift—is Michael Feinstein's "Pure Imagination." What a treat for parents and children! A bibliography of children's music is included on page 78.

Ring Around the Rosy

Materials

- Words to song

Activity

Hold hands with your child. Sing the traditional words to Ring Around the Rosy, walking slowly in a circle. When the words say, "Ashes, ashes, we all fall down," gently fall down.

As a variation, try some of the alternate verses found below. Do whatever action the verse calls for, and soon your child will let you know which is his favorite.

This is a terrific activity for including moms, dads, grandparents, and older siblings. Just caution older brothers and sisters not to yank on their younger sibling's arm.

Ring Around the Rosy

Ring around the rosy,
A pocket full of posies,
Ashes, ashes, we all fall down.

Variation 1

Run around the rosy,
A pocket full of posies,
Ashes, ashes, we all fall down.

Variation 2

Skip around the rosy,
A pocket full of posies,
Ashes, ashes, we all fall down.

Variation 3

Hop around the rosy,
A pocket full of posies,
Ashes, ashes, we all fall down.

A Kitchen Band

Materials

- Tin cups
- Pots, pans, and lids
- Wooden or stainless steel spoons

Activity

Let your two-year-old create music. Along with your child, choose some "instruments" right from the kitchen. A pot with a handle and a wooden spoon make a great drum. (A stainless steel spoon will give this instrument an entirely different sound.) Two pot lids, especially those of equal size, create a homemade xylophone when struck lightly with a spoon.

Give your child the opportunity to practice making funny sounds and singing any songs to the music she creates. You should make music right along with her.

Sing a Song

Materials

- Songs
- Songbooks
- Tapes

Activitiy

Young children love to sing. Whether it be humming along to their favorite shows, or trying to duplicate a song heard on the radio, you can never overdo singing songs with your little one. Even if you are only a shower warbler or were told in school to "please lip-sync the words," your child will think you are a virtuoso. So, learn the words and tunes to many appropriate songs. Nursery rhymes are an easy place to begin since the melodies are often familiar. A bibliography of children's music is included in this book on page 78. Check your local music store for CDs and tapes, especially those that contain lyrics that you can learn. Do not overlook show music, opera, or rock, if one of these is your favorite. Once you have learned a song, sing it for your child. Sing in the car, in the bathtub, or at the park. Make singing songs a constant activity.

Record a Song

Materials

- Tape recorder
- Blank tape
- Familiar songs

Activity

Once you have mastered a few songs, record and play them for your child. Encourage him to sing along with you. Do not be surprised when he begins singing the song or, at least, his version of it. Then, unobtrusively record him singing the song. Play it back for him and watch him delight in hearing the familiar tune.

Fill In the Words

Materials

- Lyrics to songs

Activity

Choose some songs that you especially like; ones that rhyme make this an easier activity. Then, sing the song around your child, encouraging her to sing with you. When you think she is becoming more familiar with the song, leave a word out and see if she can fill it in. Our girls' favorite was "My Favorite Things" from *The Sound of Music*. When we would sing "When the dog bites, when the . . . ," they would sing out the word "bee" with great gusto. We would then finish the line with the word "stings" amid their clapping for getting the right word. This will help language development as well as musical skills.

Teddy Bear, Teddy Bear

Materials

- Words to the poem (See below.)
- Teddy bear

Activity

Let your two-year-old pretend to be the teddy bear as you recite this poem to her. Show her the different movements that the teddy bear makes and then practice with her. Encourage her to say the words with you.

Teddy Bear, Teddy Bear

Teddy bear, teddy bear,
Turn around. (Turn slowly in a circle.)
Teddy bear, teddy bear,
Touch the ground. (Bend down and touch the ground.)
Teddy bear, teddy bear,
Show your shoe. (Pretend to show a shoe.)
Teddy bear, teddy bear,
That will do. (Shake pointer finger.)
Teddy bear, teddy bear,
Go upstairs. (Pretend to climb stairs.)
Teddy bear, teddy bear,
Say your prayers. (Fold hands together.)
Teddy bear, teddy bear,
Turn out the light. (Pretend to turn off light.)
Teddy bear, teddy bear,
Say good night. (Put hands together, rest head on them,
and say "Good night.")

Marching

Materials

- Marching music
- Marching hat

Activity

Play some marching music and have a parade with your two-year-old. Any music with a strong beat will suffice, but you may want to try some John Phillips Sousa marches. Decide where your child will have his parade. It might simply be the two of you in the kitchen, or you might want to include several other children and march in front of a few houses in the neighborhood. To add to the festivities, marchers will enjoy wearing "marching hats." Follow the simple directions below to make your own marching hats.

Marching Hats

Materials

- Full page of newspaper
- Stapler, tape, or glue
- Scissors
- Crayons or paints

Directions

1. Fold a full page of newspaper in half on the fold already provided.
2. With the fold at the top, pull the two corners down to meet in the middle. They will form two triangles, ending about two inches (5 cm) from the bottom.
3. Fold the bottom edge up on each side of the hat.
4. To make the hat sturdier and better sized for a child, cut the ends of the bottom band off and turn the band up one more time.
5. You may wish to tuck in the ends of the band and secure with a stapler, tape, or glue.
6. Let your child decorate the hat with crayons or paints.

Dancing Together

Materials

- Radio

Activity

Two-year-olds and dancing seem made for each other. Although children at this age are not yet ready for anything formal, a two-year-old can be the life of the party if the music strikes his fancy.

Choose some music that is appealing to both you and your child. This can be accomplished by turning on the radio and finding a station that plays music or by putting in a tape. Then, along with your child, start dancing. This can range from simply shaking hands up and down, to flapping your arms, and to moving your entire body.

If you have trouble moving, use your imagination. Pretend you and your child are starring at Radio City Music Hall in New York City. You are both Rockettes and are in a chorus line, holding shoulders and doing high kicks. It could be that you are in an old Fred Astaire and Ginger Rogers movie and dancing together. Or, are you dancing on *American Bandstand*? Let the music and your imagination move you. "5,6,7,8!"

One, Two, Three, Go

Materials

- Open, safe area for running

Activity

Two-year-olds love to run. Make a game of this as you teach them just a little patience and the numbers one, two, and three. Tell your child you are going to run, but she needs to wait until you count off before she starts. Then count off, "One, two, three," showing each number with your fingers. As soon as you get to three, holler "Go!" and let your child take off with you right beside her. You can stop running when you are both tired.

A Tea Party

Materials

- Words to the song
- Teacup, saucer, teapot
- Juice and cookies

Activity

The classic children's rhyme "I'm a Little Teapot" can be an enjoyable way to teach your child some manners. You may be amazed at how many times you need to repeat this song with your two-year-old. We always were! Begin by singing the song with your child. When you sing "I'm a Little Teapot," use both hands and point to yourself. When you sing "Here is my handle," put your left hand on your hip. With "And here is my spout," lift your right arm, leave it near your side, bend it at the elbow, and flop it down at the wrist. Say, "Hear me shout" very loudly. At, "Just tip me over, And pour me out," bend to the right as if tea were pouring out of the spout. When you are through with your song, you can extend the learning by having a tea party. For a two-year-old, this just means some juice and cookies. But do use either a real or doll teapot and show your child what a real handle and spout look like. Explain about the steam coming out because tea is usually served hot. Pour your "tea" into cups with saucers and enjoy your time together.

I'm a Little Teapot

I'm a little teapot,
Short and stout.
Here is my handle,
And here is my spout.
When I get all steamed up,
Hear me shout.
Just tip me over,
And pour me out.

Counting Songs and Rhymes

Materials

- Counting songs
- Stuffed animals

Activity

Your two-year-old will love to count. Although this does not have to be formal, she will soon be saying "one, two, three, four," and then more. Counting songs are fun for children to use while learning. They can be sung or recited as a poem. If you happen to have some of the animals mentioned in any of the counting rhymes, it is nice to have them be part of the reciting. Either you or your child can hold the stuffed animal and move it each time it is mentioned.

The rhymes below are among our favorites. Check out books of poetry and nursery rhymes for more of these delightful rhymes. Suggested titles can be found on page 77.

Five Little Monkeys

Five little monkeys jumping on the bed,
One fell off and bumped his head.
Mama called the doctor and the doctor said,
"No more monkeys jumping on the bed!"
Each time the verse is repeated with four, three, two, or one.

One, Two, Buckle My Shoe

One, two, buckle my shoe.
Three, four, shut the door.
Five, six, pick up sticks.
Seven, eight, lay them straight.
Nine, ten, a big fat hen.
Sounds so good, let's do it again.

ABC's

Materials

- An ABC song

Activity

At some point it is fun to introduce your two-year-old to the ABC song. It can easily be sung to the tune of "Twinkle, Twinkle, Little Star." Sing the song for him as he is in the bathtub or as you are getting him his lunch. Driving in the car is a good time for this one, too. As you sing it, encourage him to sing along. Do not expect him to really learn the letters or their sounds. At this stage he is just going to enjoy the song for the sake of singing. It may take him his whole second year and then some to even sing much past the first few letters correctly.

It is fun to show him the letters as you sing by using a magnetic board or flipping through alphabet books. Of course, everyone will comment on his precociousness. Take pride in his singing of this very important song but do remember there are other songs to learn.

ABC

(To the tune of "Twinkle, Twinkle, Little Star")
A B C D E F G,
H I J K L M N O P,
Q R S,
T U V,
W X,
Y 'n' Z.
Now I know my ABC's,
Next time won't you sing with me?

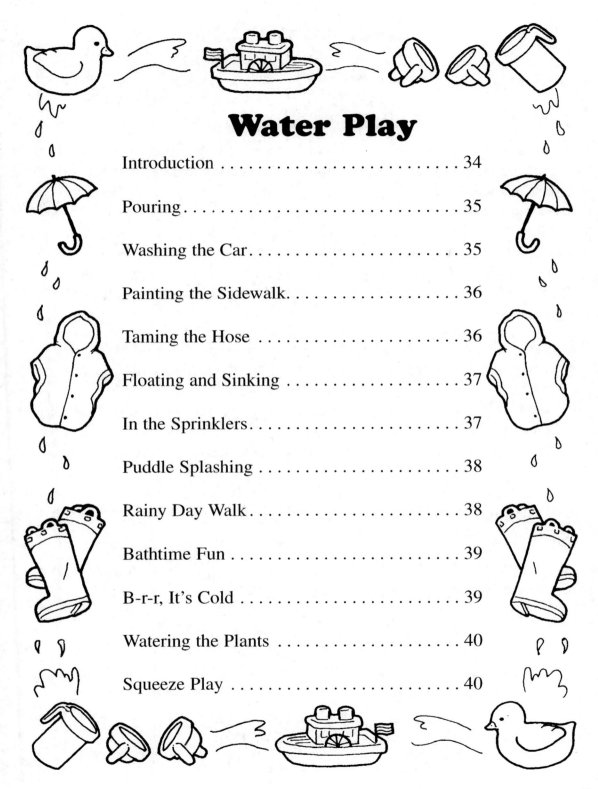

Water Play

Introduction

What is it about water that makes it so mesmerizing to two-year-olds? Is it the soothing, gentle feeling that comes with moving around in a tub full of wonderfully warm water? Is it the ripples that are produced when one throws a stone into it? Or is it the rainbows that can be seen through the sprinklers on a hot summer day? Whatever the reason, water and water play are fascinating to two-year-olds.

Water play changes each time a new container or form of water is used. The rules do not. To have fun while playing with your child, follow these simple rules:

- Never allow your child to play with, near, or in water unattended.
- Never allow your child to play with or in water that is too hot or too cold.
- Water can cause surfaces to become slippery, so keep a close eye out so our child does not slip.
- Determine if it safe for your child to drink the water before he begins to play. Not only will this be safer for him, it may save you from saying, "Do not drink the water" a countless number of times.
- Keep a towel and a change of clothes handy when letting your child play with water.

As you play with the water and your two-year-old. Keep in mind that you, too, will get wet, but it is a great way to have fun!

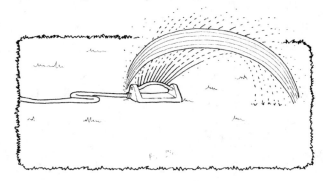

Pouring

Materials

- Water
- Non-breakable containers
- Plastic resealable bag

Activity

This activity can provide you and your two-year-old countless hours of fun. Simply pour water from one container to another. The trick is to provide as many different types of containers as you can. Cups and pitchers are obvious choices, but what about a pie pan or a plastic basket? A squeeze bottle that might have held ketchup provides endless fun while a plastic sandwich bag holds delights all its own.

You and your child can pour while she is in the bathtub, but equally as fun can be standing at the bathroom or kitchen sink or in the yard sitting on the grass.

Washing the Car

Materials

- A car
- Water
- Bucket
- Rags or sponges
- Hose
- Soap (optional)

Activity

While an adult may view washing a car as a tedious chore, a two-year-old takes great delight in helping her parent do this task. If you have a car about which you are concerned, then let your child wash her "own" ride-on toy or car while you wash your car. Regardless, do not be surprised if she gets washed instead of the car!

Give your child a rag or sponge and a bucket of water. Show her how to put the rag into the water, squeeze it out, and then how to wash the car. Our girls' special job was to make the tires shine. They would wash and rinse and dry.

Two-year-olds just think it is dandy to get to hose down the car. But this takes a patient parent willing to get very wet. One hint is to turn down the water pressure on the hose.

Painting the Sidewalk

Materials

- Bucket of water
- Paintbrushes or rollers
- Concrete surface

Activity

Let your child have the experience of using large paint brushes and rollers. Provide him with several different-sized rollers and brushes and a bucket of water. Let him paint the sidewalk or patio with them. Since the sun will dry this up, all you will need to do is pour out the water and put away the brushes and bucket. Be sure to admire your child's painting.

Safety note: Since concrete can get slippery when it is wet, keep a close eye on your child in case he wants to walk across his painting. Also, insist on rubber-soled shoes. And never leave your child unattended while he is playing with water and a bucket!

Taming the Hose

Materials

- Hose that works

Activity

Let your child have the opportunity to tame the hose. Before turning the hose on, show him where the water source begins. Let him try turning the handles and then explain that the water will soon start to come out of the hose. (It is also a good idea to remind him that he can only do this when mommy, daddy, or another grown-up is with him.) If your hose is wrapped up snake-like, take his hand and move it along the coils.

Turn the hose on very gently. Fast squirting water can frighten your child. Let him hold the hose. He will probably want to try to drink it. Have him take the clean running water, not the water from the nozzle of the hose. Once he has mastered holding the hose, let him have fun watering or moving the hose around the yard. As he gets more daring and curious, you may want to turn the water pressure up a bit. Enjoy!

Floating and Sinking

Materials

- Bathtub
- Water
- Objects that float
- Objects that sink

Activity

Little ones love to watch objects that they can push down and watch bob back up again. However, they also are fascinated by some that do not rise to the surface again. In order to make this not only a fun activity but a safe one as well, choose the items you use carefully. Test them out and make sure they are large enough for little hands to pick up easily and will not fit into your child's mouth. As your two-year-old tries to sink the object, say, "Do you think this floats or do you think it sinks?" Once the object has done one or the other, tell your child, "Oh, I see this rubber duck floats."

Good items for floating include rubber ducks, inflatable toys, boats, and wooden spoons. Good items for sinking include metal teaspoons, washcloths, and most bars of soap.

In the Sprinklers

Materials

- Sprinklers
- Dry towel

Activity

If you are lucky enough to have sprinklers available to you on a hot day, let your toddler have a treat and beat the heat. Let him run through the sprinklers—with you. The water in the sprinklers does  not have to be very high for your child to enjoy this activity, and you need not get more than your feet wet. Have your two-year-old chase you through the sprinklers and, of course, catch you; then, reverse the tables and catch him. Have a towel handy to dry off with.

Puddle Splashing

Materials

- Small puddles
- Boots

Activity

After the rain, take your child on a puddle splashing outing. Make sure she is dressed appropriately and then take off for an adventure. The puddles may be in your own front lawn or backyard, but the fun is in finding the puddles and then splashing in them. Encourage your child to kick the water, jump in, or hop in the puddles. Some children take great delight in running through the puddles. Find out your two-year-old's preference and join in the fun.

Rainy Day Walk

Materials

- A light sprinkle
- Appropriate rain gear

Activity

During a light rainfall, take your child for a rainy day walk. Make sure he is dressed appropriately in boots, raincoat, and a rain hat. Take along an umbrella in case it really starts pouring but mainly to give her an opportunity to carry it.

As you walk, talk about the rain and how it helps everything to grow. Find leaves that have large drops of water on them or point out a place where water is coming down from a building. Talk about the color of the sky. Perhaps you will be fortunate enough to see a rainbow!

Bathtime Fun

Materials

- Bathtub
- Bathtub toys

Activity

You will probably spend more time in the bathroom now than at any other time of your life, so make it fun. Let your two-year-old have lots of different bathtime toys. Although rubber ducks and boats are great fun, an old squeeze bottle or a squirt gun can bring hours of amusement. Show your child how to use the squirt gun to hit the boats and make them bob and how to use the squeeze bottle to try to sink the duck.

Every so often take the toys out and dry them off. Many times bathtub toys become smelly or slippery from the constant state of dampness.

Most importantly, never leave your child unattended in the bathtub! Even with just a little bit of water and for only a second, bathtubs are very dangerous!

B-r-r, It's Cold

Materials

- Water
- Containers
- Freezer

Activity

Let your child see what happens to water when it gets very cold. This is an especially good activity for those who do not live near the snow. Give your child a few different-sized containers and let him fill them with water and then freeze them.

Explain, but do not expect him to understand, that it takes a while for the water to freeze. When the containers are frozen, unmold them and let your child touch them and play with them. For a variation, you may want to place an object that can be frozen inside. For a special treat, make "juicesicles" with your child and have them for a snack.

Watering the Plants

Materials

- Plants
- Watering can or pitcher

Activity

Your two-year-old will enjoy helping you water the plants if you make sure she has her own watering can. The plastic type that has a secure handle and long watering spout is the easiest for a toddler to manipulate.

Talk to your child about how plants like water and sometimes need a drink. Let her know that she can help you give the plants their drink. Then, give her a partially filled watering can and take her with you to water the plants. Help her pour out the water, showing her where to place the spout. If you think she is being too generous in her watering, do not fill the can with as much water. In time, your child can water the plants on her own, if you do not mind helping wipe up occasional spills.

Squeeze Play

Materials

- Sponges
- Bowls or cake pans
- Water

Activity

Although your two will probably enjoy cleaning the table off with a damp sponge she may get just as much pleasure from squeezing a wet one. Give her a few different-sized sponges and two bowls—one with water and the other empty. Show her how to let the sponge soak up water in one bowl, move it over to the empty bowl, and squeeze it out. (Cake pans and pie tins work well for this.) Let your child have fun soaking up all the water and squeezing it out. When she is finished, show her how to change bowls and start over with the bowl she has just filled up. Maybe you will get lucky, and she will actually get some water into the bowl. We found this type of activity worked very well outside the house or sitting in an empty bathtub.

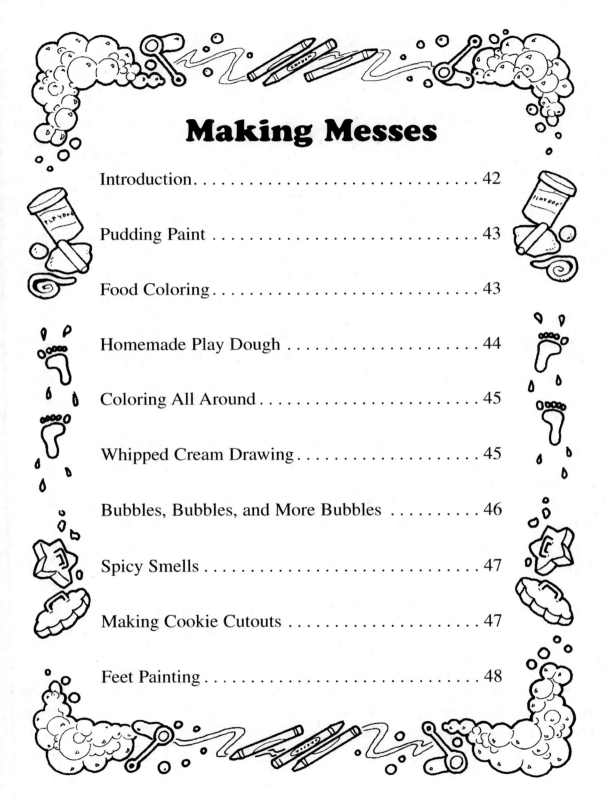

Making Messes

Introduction

Two-year-olds go hand in hand with making messes. Not only will there be clutter everywhere, there will be lots of "gooshy" stuff to contend with, as well. Try to think of the messes as learning experiences for your child. Yes, there may be a spot of paint on your ceiling, but there is also the picture that your child painted hanging on the refrigerator. Follow some of these ideas for cleanup and storage that may make the experience less frustrating.

Try to designate one area as the place where messy activities take place. If you have a playroom, perhaps it can house a child-sized table that is designated for messy use; when the weather is warm enough, an old picnic table in the backyard makes a good spot. The floor is also an alternative, one that works well when you have several children working at the same time.

Cover the work area with paper. Then, place an old, large sheet under the area. You can also use newspaper, but wet newspaper can create problems all its own. An old, plastic tablecloth works better.

Before you begin these projects, you might want to cover your child with some type of apron or smock. We found it easier to designate certain clothing as "making messes" clothing. (Dad's old dress shirts make perfect smocks.) This made getting dirty a non-issue.

Cleaning up can be a real chore. Chances are your two-year-old will not want to help. However, making it a game might work. A race to put the paper away or singing a song while storing the crayons can be motivating to a toddler.

Have sponges or cloths handy during and after project time. Two-year-old's love to wipe up, and while they may not get all the drips, it is a start. Paper towels are easiest because they can be thrown out.

As frustrating as it is to realize that you will be the one cleaning up, join your child and have a wonderful time making messes. See the project from your child's point of view. To you, the word "mess" is clearly negative, but for him it is a synonym for "fun."

Pudding Paint

Materials

- Prepared pudding
- Spoon
- Wax paper
- Masking tape

Activity

Before beginning this activity, either prepare pudding according to package directions (instant works best) or buy the already prepared type. (This is especially important if you are planning to use cooked pudding because it will need several hours to cool.) Tear off long lengths of wax paper and tape them onto the work area.

Place a few spoonfuls of pudding onto the wax paper. Then show your two-year-old how to fingerpaint in the pudding. Encourage her to make designs and swirls. Draw various shapes and show her a circle, a square, and a rectangle.

As a variation, try different flavors of pudding so you can give your child an opportunity to mix different colors.

Food Coloring

Materials

- Clear plastic cups
- Water
- Food coloring (non-toxic)

Activities

Set out two or three clear plastic cups filled with water. Help your child squirt in some food coloring. (Check the label for specific directions.) Swirl the water. Show your child how the water changes. Let him help intensify the color by adding a few more drops himself.

Try mixing different colors to see what combinations you can create. Many packages list the amounts you will need for certain colors.

You can also put a few drops of food coloring into some other liquids, such as milk or clear soda, to see what happens.

BLUE

YELLOW

GREEN

RED

Homemade Play Dough

Materials

- Mixing bowl
- 1 cup (250 mL) salt
- 1 cup (250 mL) flour
- 1/2 cup (125 mL) water
- Resealable plastic bags or bowls
- Food coloring
- Plastic cloth or place mat
- Various "tools"

Activities

In a mixing bowl, knead the salt, the flour, and the water. Add a few drops of food coloring to the dough. Store the play dough in the sealable plastic container or plastic bag. Once you have made a batch of play dough, let your two-year-old use it to be creative. Place the clay on a plastic table cloth or place mat. Let him experience the fun of just squishing it through his fingers. Talk about how this feels. Ask him if it is hard, smooth, or rough.

Play dough is an easy way to teach different shapes. Use the dough to create the shapes and then place them in front of your child and tell him what each shape is. Take his fingers and outline a square, a circle, a triangle, and a rectangle. If he wants to create his own, let him. Use the various shapes to make things, such as squares to make a house or circles and triangles to make an animal.

Fingers work really well in creating objects with the play dough, but you can increase your child's fun by adding a few tools. These can be bought commercially, but chances are your gadget drawer in the kitchen will provide many useful items. Our daughters' favorite was the garlic press that we used to make spaghetti. Cookie cutters, wire egg slicers, pastry cutters, and bottle cappers all make creative tools. As always, check to make sure these are safe and can be used by your two-year-old. Then roll up your sleeves and play right along with your little one.

Coloring All Around

Materials

- Crayons
- Blank paper
- Bucket or basket
- Tape (optional)

Activity

Provide your child with sheets of blank paper or simply cover a large area with butcher paper and let your child color anywhere on it. The "fatter" crayons are easiest for toddlers to use. Tape the butcher paper or the sheets of paper to the table to make it easier for your child to color. Keep the crayons together in one place. A plastic bucket or basket with a handle makes a convenient case for crayons.

Keep in mind that it may take awhile for your two-year-old to color more than a few marks. She may enjoy using just one color. She may not even stay on the paper. All of that is just fine as long as she enjoys her coloring.

Cleaning up crayons is rather easy to do. A paste of a mildly abrasive scouring powder will clean a surface when your child misses the paper.

Whipped Cream Drawing

Materials

- Can of whipping cream
- Plastic place mat

Activity

Place a place mat on the table. Take a can of whipped cream and squirt some on the place mat. Use the whipped cream to let your child draw. Help your little one try to squirt the whipped cream from the can. (This should only be done with your help. A child should not play with an aerosol can.) Draw his initials or his whole name.

As long as your child does not have a milk allergy, he can even taste his creation before it gets cleaned up.

Bubbles, Bubbles, and More Bubbles

Materials

- Bubble solution
- Bubble wand

Activity

Bubbles are great fun. Take turns with your child both blowing and catching bubbles. Breaking the bubbles that your child creates can be just as much fun for you as it is for your child. The little plastic bubble wand that comes in the small packages of bubbles may be plenty for your child to handle. Take some time and show him how to gently blow the bubbles. The trick is, of course, not to get them into your mouth. A word of warning: bubble solution can cause concrete to be slippery, so take care in determining where you and your two-year-old will play with bubbles.

Bubble Solution

- Large container with a lid
- 1 gallon (3.8 L) water
- 1 cup (250 mL) liquid dish detergent
- 40-60 drops of glycerin

Mix all the ingredients together. Stir well.

Bubble Wand

- Hanger
- 3 feet (.9 m) of cotton string
- Pliers
- Scissors
- Electrical or duct tape

Bend the middle section of the wire hanger into a desired shape. Twist the end sections together to form a handle. To avoid sharp edges, cover the handle with tape.

Spicy Smells

Materials

- Bowls
- Spoons
- Various spices

Activity

The spices in your pantry can provide a pleasant activity with your two-year-old. Choose two or three pleasant smelling spices. Cinnamon, cloves, and ginger work well for this. We just let our children smell them from the spice containers, but you can pour them into separate bowls if you wish. Identify the smells for your child and then mention some of the foods they are likely to smell and taste these spices in.

As an extension, you can let your child pour a little bit of each spice out onto a paper towel and try tasting it. This activity can be repeated with different spices.

Making Cookie Cutouts

Materials

- Cookie dough
- Cookie cutters
- Rolling pin
- Cookie sheet
- Flour
- Spatula
- Cookie decorations (optional)

Activity

Two-year-olds enjoy making cookies using cookie cutters. Plastic cutters that have big, simple shapes will cause the least amount of frustration because they will not have intricate cutouts. If you do not have cookie cutters, plastic drinking glasses will make a fine substitute.

Prepare or purchase dough for making cutout cookies. Cover the work surface with flour. Then, use the rolling pin to flatten the dough. Do not roll it thicker than 1/2 inch (1.25 cm). Next, show your child how to put the cookie cutter into the flour and cut the dough. Help him use the spatula to lift the cookie onto the cookie sheet.

Depending on how interested he is, you might want to decorate the cookies before you bake them.

Feet Painting

Materials

- Butcher paper
- Finger paints
- Pie or cake pan
- Towels or wipes

Activity

Take a long piece of butcher paper. Place it in an area that will allow your child some movement and that can be easily cleaned, such as a strip of grass or in the bathtub. You might want to dress your child in shorts or a bathing suit.

Pour some paint into the bottom of the cake pan. (There should be enough paint to cover the bottom of your child's feet.) Place the pan close to the butcher paper. Help your child place his feet into the pan, slowly, one foot at a time. Have him lift one foot and let the paint on it drip into the pan. Then, place this foot on the paper. Repeat with the second foot. Now, let your child paint with his feet. Let him walk back and forth on the paper or move around in circles. Encourage him to create patterns or to take giant steps to vary the size of the spaces in between. You can help him wipe off his feet and step into another pan of paint. If you are really brave you can have him step into two different colors at the same time.

Let the butcher-paper-art dry. It makes wonderful gift wrapping for someone special in your two-year-old's life.

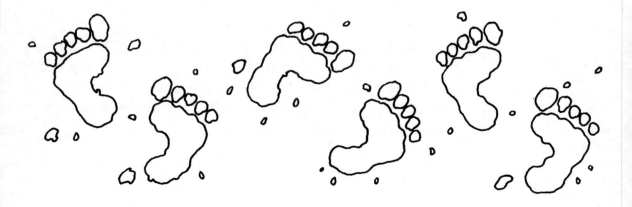

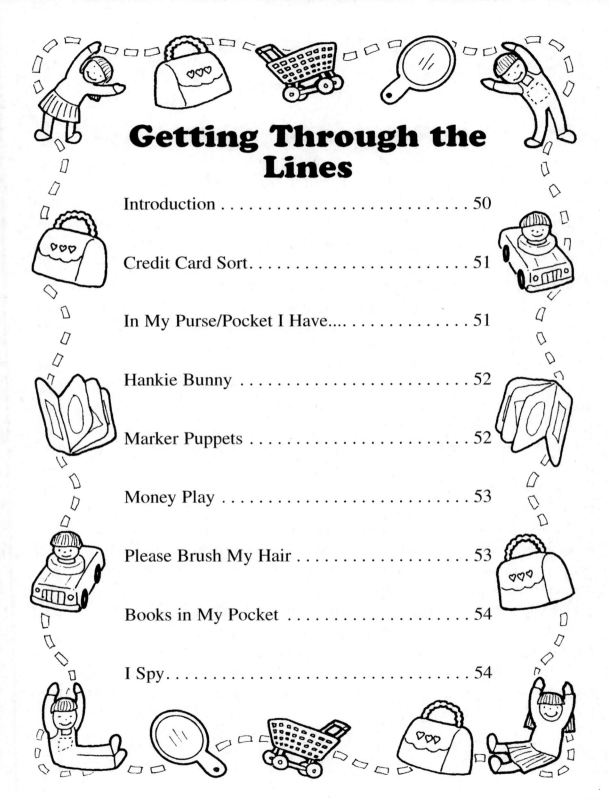

Getting Through the Lines

Introduction

There are so many times that you will have to wait with your two-year-old. It might be when you are checking out at the grocery store or at the doctor's office waiting to be seen. Perhaps your older child has a program at school and you and your toddler are waiting for the curtain to rise. At some time in your child's second year of life, you will have to entertain her while waiting.

The activities in this section are intended to help make those moments a bit easier. Many of these activities require only the things that you normally carry with you in a purse, pocket, or diaper bag; they put a new spin on the ordinary. Others require things you might want to pack just in case. Finally, some activities use items commonly found in places where we wait.

It seems that waiting is never really fun, but if you are prepared it might be better than you think. We always made sure there were not only lots of things to do that required little preparation or thinking on our part but also special snacks reserved for waiting times.

Check out where you are. Can you and your two-year-old get up and move around before you are called in? Is there a strip of lawn you can run on before your appointment? Check it out and then do some running games. (See page 20.)

Only you will know how long your child can wait. You may run out of ideas before your turn arises, but with a little preparation and some special snacks, waiting may be a breeze. To avoid an overwhelming situation, do not wait until your child fusses to begin to play.

However, if your child gets fussy, try to keep calm. In a pinch, you may have to go to the head of the line and ask to be served first. You may be surprised what others will allow so they do not have to hear a squalling two-year-old. As a last resort, you may even have to give up and go home. But before this, try the activities in this section and see if getting through the line isn't easier than you think.

Credit Card Sort

Materials

- Credit cards

Activity

If you carry credit cards in your wallet this is one of the easiest games you will play with your child. Put a few credit cards out in front of your child. A young two-year-old may do no more than sort through them and stack them up. An older child can put them into some type of order that you show him. Perhaps you have two gold-colored cards. He can put those two together. You can show him your name on a few and have him find others with your name. You can create your own games with any characteristics that credit cards have in common, such as lettering, logos, colors, and numbers.

This game will keep your two-year-old amused for quite a while if you do not give him all the cards at one time. Our girls liked taking them out of our wallets as well as putting them back in. It almost never failed to work at the restaurant table when the service was slow.

In My Purse/Pocket I Have...

Materials

- Objects or toys

Activity

Before going someplace where you anticipate a wait, look around your house and put some things into your purse or pocket that your child will be excited to see. A favorite book or catalog, little cards, small cars, or a new box of crayons and a small pad of paper are easy to transport and will be welcomed by your little one. He will be surprised and delighted to see one of his favorites in a new and unusual setting. Some things can best be played with at a table and a chair, so consider where you will be before you pack up.

Hankie Bunny

Materials

- Marker
- Handkerchief

Activity

The big handkerchiefs work best for this. Always carry a few with you. Even if you do not make bunnies with them, you can put one on your head and amuse your child that way. To make a "hankie bunny," simply pull the handkerchief in a ball in your hand then put up two ears. In truth, unless you are using a starched handkerchief, this will look like a lop-eared rabbit, but your two will not mind. Take the marker and make two dots for the eyes and a line for the mouth. Then, proceed to let the bunny talk to your child. Your bunny might tell your child what you are waiting for or what you will do when you are through. When you are done, you can make the bunny go through the bunny hole by putting your opposite hand on your hip and putting the bunny through the hole. Hopefully by this time, your waiting time will be up.

Marker Puppets

Materials

- Fine-tipped marker

Activity

They are so simple to create, take only a minute to do, and provide lots of amusement. All you need to do is take a marker and put faces on your fingers. Your thumbs and index finger will work the best. You need dots for the eyes and nose and a line for the mouth. Your puppets can tell stories or talk to your two-year-old. You can even make marker puppets on your child's fingers and have him try making his puppets talk.

Money Play

Materials

- Coins

Activity

You probably have some coins in your pocket or purse. These can fill hours of waiting time. Let your child hold the coins. Allow her to take them out of your change purse and put them back in. Let her stack them up and knock them down again. Show her how to sort them by type.

She can also make faces with the coins. Let her help you make a circle out of coins and then use different coins to make the parts of the face. As she puts a coin down to represent the eyes, ask her to find her eyes. Repeat this for each part of her face.

See if you can get the coins to spin. She will enjoy watching them turn and might even successfully get one to turn after lots and lots of practice.

Just remind her that money should never go near her mouth and, of course, keep a watchful eye.

Please Brush My Hair

Materials

- Hair brush or comb
- Mirror (optional)

Activity

Of course, you have brushed your two-year-old's hair four times before leaving today. Why would you need to brush it again? You do not, but your little one might take great pleasure in brushing yours. It is something that may take up a few minutes, especially if the two of you take turns brushing each other's hair. This becomes even more fun when you use two different hair brushes and add a mirror into the mix to check the results. (This is probably not a good activity before a major business appointment or at a dinner table!)

Books in My Pocket

Materials

• Small board books

Activity

With so many little books on the market today it is not too difficult to pack a few books away to use while waiting someplace. Always take a few tried and true favorites, but often times it is the new ones that will capture your little one's attention, especially if you allow him to hold the book when through. Our girls really liked little board books for the times they had to wait. They were very brightly colored with very little text, and they enjoyed turning the pages.

I Spy

Materials

• None

Activity

This works well if your child is someplace where he can move around a little bit. In the traditional game you give clues, eventually revealing what you are looking at. For a two-year-old this game can be simplified a bit. For example, say to him, "I see a picture on the wall. Do you see the picture? Can you show Mommy the picture?" If your child sees the picture, he can walk over to it and point it out to you. If he cannot find it, walk over to the picture together and say, "This is the picture that Mommy saw."

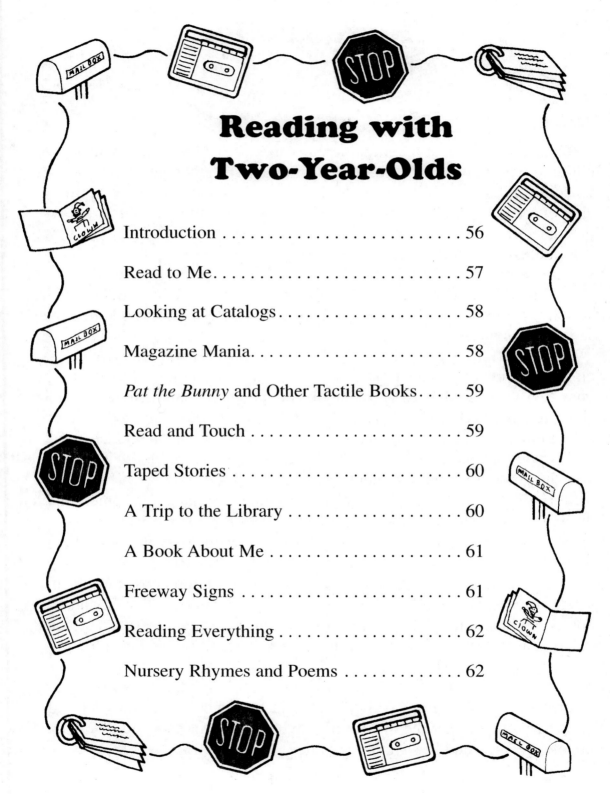

Reading with Two-Year-Olds

Introduction

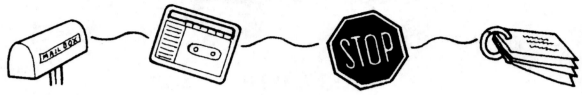

Research shows that reading to babies and toddlers produces young children who become avid readers. If nothing else, they get to practice listening skills as very little children. This is no mean feat, if you think about it from an adult perspective. Sitting and listening take time and patience.

Reading does more than teach reading skills; it opens up the world. Reading aloud gives little ones the chance to hear language as well as rhythm and rhyme. They can begin very early on to see a link between the written and the spoken word. Pictures fill their lives as they see beyond what they see in their own worlds.

Reading affords you and your child a very special opportunity for closeness and communication. What better way to snuggle with your very busy two-year-old than to grab a book and a blanket, cuddle together in a big chair, and read? With each book shared, you are undertaking a different adventure. You are introducing your child to new people and places. The words you read are helping your child increase her vocabulary. The pictures you show her create new sights for her to see.

Story time in many families becomes a ritual. Perhaps it is something you do first thing in the morning or just before bedtime. When you first get home from work, reading a book together gives you a few moments to reconnect.

There are literally thousands of books from which to choose. You can select story books, wordless books, bathtub books, pop-up books, and shape books. Be sure that you include some of your favorite nursery rhymes and poems, fairy tales, and a few classics. Keep in mind that your child may have one story that she favors.

Books make wonderful gifts. Encourage family members and friends to add to your growing library. If you read just one book a day to your child, one year will give her the opportunity to hear 365 stories—and give you 365 opportunities to cuddle. Happy reading!

Read to Me

Materials

• Several books (See page 77.)

Activity

Reading to a child can bring great joy to both of you if you respect your little one's ability to listen. You may have a child who can sit through a whole story and then ask for more, or you may have one who makes it through two pages and has had enough. Whichever your child chooses to do, respect him and do not push him to do more than he can handle. When he is ready to listen, he will.

Reading to a two-year-old usually means "close time." This is accomplished by placing your toddler on your lap or next to you. Select a book together. You can often guide him to a story which you enjoy. If you do not enjoy the story, it will show in how you read it. However, for your child's sake, try to show some enthusiasm, even if it is the 40th time you have read the story.

Read with expression in your voice, varying the pitch for various characters. Encourage your child to look at the words and pictures with you. You may occasionally point out a certain word or letter as you read. When you are through, ask your child a few questions about the story. "Did you like the train in the story?" "What did the family eat for dinner?" As your child gets older, try to ask a few questions that do not have a yes or no answer. Give him time to think of the answers before you answer for him.

Looking at Catalogs

Materials

• Catalogs

Activity

If you are fortunate, you will get lots of catalogs in the mail. Check your mailbox regularly and keep every catalog that comes into the house. You may want to keep them in a special place that is easily accessible to your little one. Then, when you have a few minutes, sit down with your two-year-old and look at a catalog together. Read some of the descriptions of what is being sold. You do not have to read every word, but start to encourage your child to show you where on the page she sees the yellow raincoat or the toy train set.

Two-year-olds rarely tire of catalogs as they get older. Keep your supply updated, tossing out the dog-eared copies and replacing them with new ones. If you do not receive catalogs, read a magazine and find a product you might be interested in and call their 800 number to order the catalog.

Magazine Mania

Materials

• Magazine with lots of pictures

Activity

It never fails. Just as you think you have a minute and sit down to read a magazine, your child joins you. Make this a time to play and learn together. Tell her you are about to read a magazine. Explain what a magazine is. Keep it very simple. "A magazine is a group of stories about different things. It has advertising and pictures in it." Then show her the magazine, pointing out the pictures and ads. Be careful. You may need to preview the magazine before you choose to show your child any pictures from it.

Pat the Bunny and Other Tactile Books

Materials

- Tactile books (See page 77.)

Activity

Reading with your wiggly two-year-old can sometimes be trying. If your child desires a more interactive experience, try a tactile book. These are books that include different textures which your child can touch as you read. The stories are written so that touching is encouraged. *Pat the Bunny* is one such classic book.

To extend the learning from the book, begin to make connections with your child. If the material your two-year-old is touching is soft, ask him, "What else do we touch that is soft?" When you are through with your reading session, do not forget some of the textures that you both felt in the book. Throughout the course of the day, when you find something soft, give it to your child to feel. Ask him, "How does this feel? Is it soft like the bunny in the book?"

Read and Touch

Materials

- Thick paper
- Rings
- Hole punch
- Scissors
- Tape or glue
- Marker
- Textured materials

Activity

Make your own texture book by collecting all types of textured materials. (Examples include cotton balls, sand paper, carpet squares, and crumpled tin foil.) Fabrics and papers work well for this, but do not limit yourself. You may find something else that is just perfect. Use construction paper or large index cards and secure the textured material onto the paper. With a marker, write a label for the texture, such as bumpy, soft, or slippery. Punch holes into the sides of the cards and put rings through them. Then, sit, read, and touch this texture book with your child.

Taped Stories

Materials

- Tape recorder
- Blank tapes
- Stories

Activity

Once you have recorded some of her favorite stories, your two-year-old will be able to enjoy a story anytime. While you are reading to her, tape record one or two of her favorite stories. Begin by saying, "This is Helena's mommy. I am going to read the story *Kitty's Paint Brush* especially for Helena." Then, record the story for her.

These taped stories are especially good to listen to while driving in the car or when you go out and leave your child with someone else.

A Trip to the Library

Materials

- Public library
- Book bag or container

Activity

Since you can never have too many books, the public library can be a tremendous help. If you do not already have a library card, now is the time to get one.

Go to the library often. It can be a most exciting place for a two-year-old to explore. Many libraries have special areas for children's books. If you are in a quandary about what books to check out, ask the librarian. Check out several books. Our only problem was remembering to return all the library books, so we brought the same book bag or container each time and counted the number of books we were checking out.

While you are visiting the library ask about special programs for children. Some libraries provide puzzles and games for your child so you will have a chance to browse yourself. Others have a story time for toddlers. We tried to make the library a second home for our children. Now, they still enjoy going to the library.

A Book About Me

Materials

- Thick paper
- Rings
- Hole punch
- Scissors
- Tape or glue
- Photos of your child

Activity

Your child will enjoy reading a story starring herself. You will need photos of her. Glue them onto index cards or construction paper and then write a story featuring your child. Do not be intimidated by the fact that you have to write the story. The text should be very simple and can describe the pictures. It can be fun to use pictures from a particular trip or outing to create a story. Your child will enjoy hearing her name. For example:

> Page 1: This is Joanna in her stroller.
> Page 2: Here is Joanna in the rose garden.
> Page 3: Joanna is taking a nap.
> Page 4: We are visiting our friends in Oregon.

As an alternative to cutting and pasting, you can place the pictures into a photo album and put the text underneath the pictures.

Freeway Signs

Materials

- Road signs

Activity

As you drive along on freeways or highways, begin to point out large road signs to your child. When you exit, read the sign to your child and say, "This is our exit. It is Rosecrans. Rosecrans begins with an R." Your child will begin to understand that Rosecrans is the exit you take to go home and will eventually begin to recognize the name and the letter R.

Reading Everything

Materials

- Anything with a label

Activity

As adults we know that reading is a lifelong skill that is useful for more than reading a book. Your child has no concept of this, so become a model by reading everything. When you sit down at the table for breakfast, show her the cereal box and read the label. Point out the words and what they say. When you put the detergent in the washing machine, read what it says. If you put a tape into the tape player, read the selections out loud to your child. Anything that can be read counts.

Nursery Rhymes and Poems

Materials

- Words to nursery rhymes and poems
- (See page 77, and Music and Movement section.)

Activity

Reading nursery rhymes and poems to two-year-olds is a delightful way to spend time together. Choose a few that you really enjoy, especially those that you remember from your childhood. Find them in a book that is brightly illustrated. Sit with your child and read them together. As your two-year-old grows, he will start to understand the sound of the rhyming words and will say them with you.

Find some of the lesser known rhymes. These are often great fun and provide for some great entertainment as your two-year-old starts to remember them.

Here again is another opportunity to stretch your child's vocabulary since many old rhymes use words differently than we do today. Our older child loved the rhyme "Lucy Locket Lost Her Pocket." She was amazed to find out that a pocket was not what she thought but more like a purse.

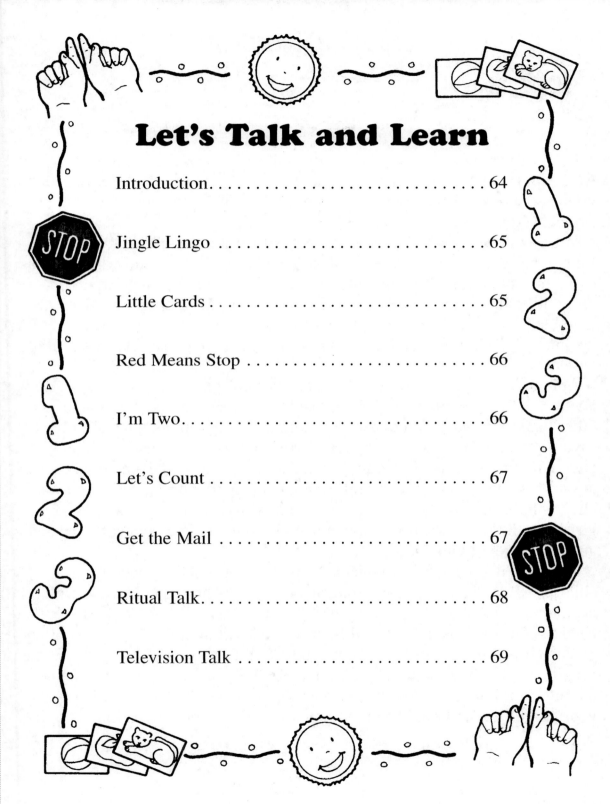

Let's Talk and Learn

Introduction

Just last year your two-year-old only smiled and gurgled in response to what you said. Now he is responding with words. His no's are delivered with resounding feeling and his yes's are often followed with a winning smile. The joy of communication!

You can now begin to have wonderful conversations with your child. Remember when he was little and you did all the talking? Now the time has come for you to not only talk but to do something that is often infinitely more difficult—listen. Listening is easy, you say. How could it possibly be a problem to listen to my own child? Because a two-year-old is just beginning to put words and thoughts together, listening takes a great deal of patience.

Although he can now tell you he wants milk or juice, he does have to think about it before he tells you. It is probably easier to just give him one or the other than to wait for him to ask. It might be hard to break the habit of saying, "You want juice." However, if you start to put words into your child's mouth, you will be doing him a disservice. He needs the time to answer. As adults, we process information so much more quickly, and we already have the vocabulary in place. Your two-year-old does not. When our girls were little, we learned to count silently to ten before we even expected an answer from them.

As adults it is also our responsibility to model useful language for children. If you want your child to speak in complete sentences, you will need to do this. If you constantly use "baby talk," so will your child. You need to consider this, as you will be the speaker your child hears most often.

Since it is often difficult to just begin talking to your two-year-old, use the activities in this section to help him not only talk but also to learn as he is talking. They are intended to open the lines of communication early on in your child's life and establish the foundation for lifelong verbal interaction.

Jingle Lingo

Materials

- Rhymes or jingles from commercials or products

Activity

Regardless of your feelings about television or radio, your child is going to come into contact with them. Use the jingles from various products to increase your two-year-old's vocabulary. As you are watching television or listening to the radio, be aware of the catchy jingles. Say or sing them with your child. Talk about what some of the words mean. Then, encourage your child to sing them herself. Both the rhythm, the music, and the words will help her learn and increase her vocabulary.

Little Cards

Materials

- Index cards
- Scissors
- Tape or glue
- Pictures from magazines or boxes

Activity

Take a bit of time to create little cards for your two-year-old to look at and talk about with you. Find pictures that you like and cut them out. Good sources of pictures that toddlers enjoy talking about include magazines, cereal cartons, and boxes that toys come in. After you have cut the pictures out, secure them to the index cards.

Sit down with your child and show her the cards, one at a time. Talk about what you see in the picture, "Oh, I see a kitty. She looks like our kitty." Encourage your child to talk about what she sees on the cards. With a young two-year-old you may only get one word answers, but as she grows you will be surprised what your two sees in the pictures that you have missed.

Store the pictures in a handy spot so they are readily accessible when you have just a moment to sit with your child. Keeping a set of little cards in your purse or pocket makes this a ready-made game for those times you have to wait with your little one.

Red Means Stop

Materials
• Street signs

Activity

As you take your child for a ride in the car or a walk down the street, start to point out the traffic signs. Stop signs are perfect for this because they are large and red. Each time you come to a stop sign, say, "Red means stop. Do you see the red stop sign?" Of course, stopping the car or your walk will help emphasize this. When you stop at a red light, also explain that the red in the light means the same as a street sign. **Safety Note:** Even as your two-year-old begins to make connections with the colors and the words, do not expect him to really understand about stopping and going.

I'm Two

Materials
• None

Activity

You will not have enough fingers and toes to keep track of the number of times that someone asks your child, "How old are you?" It will delight the questioner to hear your child gleefully respond, "I'm two." Begin to help him learn the answer to this question right around his second birthday. This way when someone questions him at his birthday party, even if he does not respond verbally, he will recognize the question.

Also show him what the number two looks like. Physically, it is difficult for most two-year-olds to hold up the index and third finger. An easier alternative for teaching a young two is to hold up the index finger on one hand and then the index finger on the other and place them side by side. We can still see our daughters gleefully screaming "I'm two" and bumping their index fingers together at every opportunity.

Let's Count

Materials
• None

Activity
Learning to talk and count seem to go hand in hand. Make counting a game to help your child learn. As you walk upstairs ask, "How many stairs do you think there are?" Then hold hands and count them as you go. In the grocery store look at the shelves of canned goods. Choose one item and count them with your child. Go slowly so your child can catch on. As he becomes more able to count, leave out a number and see if he can say it. Start with no more than 1 through 10, and do not be surprised if he gets them mixed up for a long time. The more often you repeat this game, the easier saying the words will be for him.

Get the Mail

Materials
• Mail

Activity
Letting your two-year-old take the mail in from the mailbox is really a treat. Once you reach the mailbox, let her take all the mail out. Teach her to look at each piece, and then hand them over to you. As you get each piece tell her who it is for. If she has something addressed to her, be sure to point out her name. If there are magazines, talk about what they contain. When you are inside with the mail, take a look at these magazines with her.

On some days you may receive only junk mail. This will be the biggest treat for your child. The ads from the toy stores and the envelopes filled with coupons will give you and your child lots to talk about. The most fun for your little one is that she can keep this mail for her very own. And since she will enjoy them, you will finally realize there is a reason you receive those unsolicited catalogs!

Ritual Talk

Activity

It is important to teach your two-year-old about order. A morning talk can become a ritual that not only enhances your two-year-old's speech and puts some order into his day but also becomes an enjoyable way to begin each morning. After your morning hugs, kisses, and cuddles, create a list of statements and questions to share with your child. As this routine is established, your two-year-old will look forward to hearing the same questions each morning. Although in the beginning you may be doing both the asking and the answering, as your little one grows he will begin to do both.

Materials

• None

Begin each morning by asking or saying:

1. What day is it?
   Today is Tuesday.

2. What is today's date?
   It is June 2nd.

3. Let's look out the window. What do you see?
   Oh, I see our tree. It has lots of green leaves.

4. Is it raining or sunny?
   It is sunny this morning.

5. Is it cold or warm?
   It is warm. You can wear shorts today.

6. Are there clouds in the sky?
   It is clear this morning.

Television Talk

Materials

- Television set

Activity

Regardless of your feelings about television, it will probably happen that your two-year-old will become enthralled with the moving pictures and sound coming from that box. Although you will want to restrict television watching, you can make television an ally in learning language.

Choose television shows with care. There is some excellent children's programming. Sometimes videos, since you can control them, are a better choice for young viewers.

Watch the chosen show with your child. Once the show is over, ask your child questions about what you watched together.

When big brother or sister comes home from school, have him or her question the younger sibling about the day. This is a great way to include the older child in the two-year-old's life. A five- or ten-year-old will have different sorts of things to discuss than you do. You will be surprised at how quickly your little one will be asking the older sibling about his or her day!

If you have a neighbor who is often home and likes to talk to children, take advantage of him or her. A child who hears different people talk will develop a better grasp of language. Other people have different phrasing, vocabulary, and dialects that will encourage your child to think about language in special ways. They may be reticent about answering back at the beginning, but if the neighbor is patient, your youngster will soon be willing to have conversations with others.

Let's Pretend

Introduction

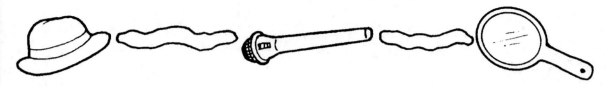

Playing dress-up, pretending to ride a horse, or having a conversation as she puts her baby to bed are all examples of how a two-year-old will play pretend.

Pretending is the art of letting your imagination take over and two-year-old's are really terrific at this. As parents, we can learn a lot if we take our cues from our little ones and let our imaginations roam. For those of us who live in the real world, it may feel silly putting on a floppy hat or having a pretend snack of juice and crackers, but it is through this type of play that we can see ourselves in our children. When we take the time to sing songs or read stories to our children as they go to bed, we may well get to watch them imitate us and do the same with their dolls. When was the last time you got down on all fours and pretended to be a lion who growled and roared? Your two-year-old will have a dandy time if you imagine yourself in the jungle or on a farm. Let him show off all he knows about animal sounds and movement.

Props for imaginative dramatic play are very useful. Sometimes they are hats or dishes, but blocks and balls are terrific, too. Blocks, especially, can be turned into so many things. Add a few play people, animals, or cars and you have a farm, a freeway, a grocery store, a forest, a park, or a zoo. It may be that you have to set the stage by suggesting ways to pretend, but as your child does more, it will become something that he does often.

While commercial play kitchens and work benches are wonderful toys for imaginative play, so are boxes of all kinds that quickly become stoves and sawhorses. Baskets, pots and pans, or just about any item that your child can imagine as something else, will be used in pretend play. When our girls were little, we drank lots of pretend tea and cookies, went to the petting zoo with stuffed animals, and went on many bear hunts, all in our living room. Watching our children pretend, playing with them while they did, and then realizing how rich their imaginations were, we had as much fun as they did.

Dress-Up

Materials

- Large clothing
- Full-length mirror (optional)

Activity

Your little one will have a great time playing dress-up. Choose clothing that is easy to get in and out of, like hats, purses, and shoes. Things that buckle and tie can create a problem, as can anything that is too long. A cowboy hat and a vest may be all it takes for him to begin pretending to be someone else. Instead of just admiring your child, dress up with him. Put on a hat and create some kind of scenario to go along with your costumes. Let your child admire how he looks in a full length mirror as he pretends to be whomever he wants to be.

Feed the Baby

Materials

- Dolls or stuffed animals
- Spoon
- Bowl
- Cup

Activity

Your two-year-old puts a high priority on eating, so this game is a natural for him. Let him pretend to feed the baby or the stuffed animals. He can do this with a baby bowl and spoon, doll dishes, or the real thing. If he still has his own high chair, perhaps he can put the baby into it so that he can really feed him. The older your two-year-old is, the more he will enjoy this. However, even more fun than feeding the baby will be the opportunity to pretend to feed you. Your child might even want to add a cup to the feeding set so you can have a drink, as well.

Blocks for Play

Materials

- Blocks
- Dolls
- Other play toys

Activity

Blocks make one of the most important props that your child can have when playing pretend games. A simple square block can become a car, a pillow for a doll, or a plate of food. Encourage your child to play with blocks when remembering the day you spent at the beach or the trip you took to grandma's.

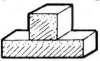

Ride 'em Horsy

Materials

- Empty gift wrap rolls

Activity

Let your two-year-old pretend to ride a horse. Give her an empty roll from gift paper and show her how to ride her horsy. Teach her to say "Giddyap," and she may just take off down the road. You might enjoy saddling up with her and going for a ride yourself.

Can You Do What I Do?

Materials

- None

Activity

This is a pretend game because you begin by pretending to be something like a bird. You then say to your two-year-old, "Look at me, I'm a bird. I can flap my wings. Can you?" Then proceed to "flap your wings." Your child will try to imitate what you do. Choose all kinds of animals such as a lion that growls or a fish that swims. This will give your two-year-old opportunities to pretend to be something other than himself.

I'm the Star

Materials

- Music
- Microphone (optional)

Activity

Give your child the chance to pretend to be the star of a show. You can be the audience or you can participate and be part of the act. Let your child pretend to sing along with any song. (She may surprise you and start really singing.) Using a real or pretend microphone makes this more fun. Encourage your child to sing into the microphone and perform. The two of you can sing a song for siblings. Encourage the rest of the family to join in.

Telephone Play

Materials

- Play or real telephone

Activity

Your two-year-old has been watching you and probably interrupting you on the telephone for several months. If he does not have his own telephone, now is the time to get him a make-believe one. If you buy him a play one, make sure the cord is much too short to wrap around his neck. If you give him a real telephone, it is best to disconnect the cord from it.

Encourage your child to talk on his pretend telephone. You can even pretend it is ringing, pick it up, and then hand it to him, telling him it is Grandma or Grandpa on the phone. Then, encourage him to have a conversation with the caller.

For more fun, get a second play phone and have conversations with your toddler.

Play Place

Materials

- Special area

Activity

Your child will increase his world of pretend play by creating special play places in your home. Perhaps he will want to play under the table and pretend it is a cave. A spot behind the couch that only he can reach may be a park or seaside. Let him have this special spot for himself, especially if there are other siblings who will insist on being in his space all the time. We have seen two-year-olds make their own space in the playpen that they would have nothing to do with as babies. If he invites you into this area, then you may go; otherwise, you should respect it as his territory.

Paper Bag Puppets

Materials

- Lunch sacks
- Markers or crayons

Activity

With a marker, draw faces and bodies on two lunch sacks. Make sure the mouth is at the crease so it will open and close when "speaking." Help your child decorate the puppet. Put the sack on your hand and make it talk. Show your child how to do this and then have a dialogue with the puppets. Your puppets can talk to each other or tell stories. Let everyone in the family make a puppet and see how much fun you'll have.

Bibliography

Resources

These books may serve as a resource when trying to find out more about your child.

Allison, Christine. *I'll Tell You a Story, I'll Sing You a Song.* Dell, 1987.

Ames, Louise. *Your Two-Year-Old: Terrible or Tender.*

Blaustine, Jan. *The Joy of Parenthood.* Simon and Schuster, 1993.

Brazelton, T. Berry, M.D. *Touchpoints.* New York: Addison Wesley, 1992.

Caplan, Theresa and Frank. *The Early Childhood Years: The 2 to 6 Year Old.* Putnam, 1983.

Decker, Celia Anita. *Children: The Early Years.* The Goodheart-Willcox Co., Inc., 1991.

Fisher, John, J. (ed.) *Johnson and Johnson—From Baby to Toddler.* Putnam, 1988.

Jessel, Camilla. *From Birth to Three.* Bantam Doubleday Dell, 1990.

Kelly, Marguerite & Elia Parsons. *The Mother's Almanac.* Doubleday, 1975.

Leach, Penelope. *Your Baby and Child, from Birth to Age 5.* Dorling Kindersley, Inc., 1989.

Riverside Mother's Group. *Don't Forget the Rubber Ducky.*

Ryder, Verdene. *Parents and their Children.* Adams-Hall, 1993.

Silver, Susan. *Baby's Best.* Simon and Schuster, 1995.

Spock, Dr. Benjamin, M.D., & Michael Rothenberg, M.D. *Dr. Spock's Baby and Child Care.* Simon and Schuster, 1992.

Trelease, Jim. *The New Read-Aloud Handbook.* Penguin, 1989.

White, Burton. *First Three Years of Life.* Simon and Schuster, 1995.

Bibliography

Children's Books

Ahlberg, Janet, & Allan Ahlberg. *Peek-a-boo!* Puffin, 1981.

Arnold, Tedd. *No Jumping on the Bed.* Dial, 1987.

Bliss, Phil (illustrator). *Kidsongs Around the World.* Publication International, 1995.

Brown, Margaret Wise. *Baby Animals.* Random, 1989.

Brown, Margaret Wise. *Goodnight Moon.* Harper, 1947.

Brown, Ruth. *Our Cat Flossie.* Dutton, 1986.

Carle, Eric. *Do You Want to Be My Friend?* Putnam, 1971.

Carle, Eric. *The Very Hungry Caterpillar.* Putnam, 1986.

dePaola, Tomie (illustrator). *Tomie dePaola's Mother Goose.* Putnam, 1987.

Dunn, Phoebe. *Busy, Busy, Toddler.* Random House, 1987.

Eastman, P. D. *Are You My Mother?* Random House, 1960.

Freeman, Don. *Courduroy.* Puffin, 1976.

Hague, Michael (illustrator). *Teddy Bear, Teddy Bear: A Classic Action Rhyme.* Morrow, 1993.

Hill, Eric. *Spot.* Puffin, 1988. In the same series: *Where's Spot?* and *Spot Goes to the Beach.*

Jensen, Patricia. *My House.* Children's Press, 1990.

Kunhardt, Dorothy. *Pat the Bunny.* Golden, 1962.

Lowerey, Jannette S. *The Pokey Little Puppy.* Golden, 1942.

McCloskey, Robert. *Make Way for Ducklings.* Puffin, 1976.

Oxenbury, Helen. *I Can.* Candlewick Press, 1985. In the same series: *I Hear and I See.*

Oxenbury, Helen. *Tickle, Tickle.* Macmillan, 1987. In the same series: *All Fall Down, Clap Hands,* and *Say Goodnight.*

Ricklin, Neil. *Daddy and Me.* Simon and Schuster, 1988. In the same series: *Mommy and Me* and *Grandpa and Me.*

Salt, Jane. *First Words for Babies and Toddlers.* Random House, 1990.

Sharon, Lois, & Bram, Staff. Sharon, Lois, and Bram's *Mother Goose: Songs, Finger Rhymes, Tickling Verses, Games, and More.* Little, 1986.

Turkle, Brinton. *Deep in the Forest.* Dutton, 1976.

Wood, Audrey. *The Napping House.* Harcourt, 1984.

Wright, Blanche Fisher (illustrator). *Real Mother Goose.* Checkerboard.

Zelinsky, Paul O. (adapted by). *The Wheels on the Bus.* Dutton, 1990.

Bibliography

CDs and Tapes

Many recordings found on CD can also be found on tape, although not as readily.

A Child's Celebration of Showtunes. (Cassette) Music for Little People. Warner Brothers Records, Inc. 1992–1993.

Barney's Favorites. (Cassette) Lyons Partnership, 1993.

Disney (Almost all Disney music is appropriate—here are some of our family favorites.)

Beauty and the Beast, Soundtrack (CD)

Classic Disney. (Cassette)

Disney Children's Favorite, Volumes 1–4. (Cassette) (These can be purchased as a set.)

My First Sing-Along, Favorite Nursery Rhymes. (Cassette)

Simply Mad About the Mouse. (Cassette)

Feinstein, Michael. *Pure Imagination.* (CD) Elektra, 1992.

Lewis, Shari. *Lambchop Sing-Along.* (CD) A&M, 1988.

Raffi. *Baby Beluga.* (CD) Troubadour Records, 1982.

Raffi. *Banannaphone.* (CD) Troubadour Records, 1994.

Raffi. *Rise and Shine.* (CD) Troubadour Records, 1982.

Reggae and Calypso Music for Kids. *Smilin' Island of Songs.* (Cassette) Music for Little People, 1992–1993. Warner Brothers Records, Inc.

Sesame Street Celebrates. (Cassette) Children's Television Workshop, 1994.

Sharon, Lois, and Bram. (Cassette) *The Elephant Show.* Drive Entertainment, 1994.